MATERIALS *and* MATTER

MAKING SENSE *of* **SCIENCE**

Peter Riley

A$^+$
Smart Apple Media

First published in 2004 by Franklin Watts
96 Leonard Street, London EC2A 4XD

Franklin Watts Australia
45–51 Huntley Street, Alexandria NSW 2015

Series editor: Rachel Cooke, Editors: Kate Newport and
Andrew Solway, Art director: Jonathan Hair, Designer: Mo Choy,
Picture research: Diana Morris

Picture credits:
Dr. Jeremy Burgess/Science Photo Library: 23c. Mark Edwards/Still
Pictures: front cover main, 1. Firepix/Topham: 13t, 18. Simon Fraser/
Science Photo Library: 29b. Bob Krist/Corbis: 25br. Imagestate/Alamy: 4.
Andrew Lambert Photographs/Science Photo Library: 15cl. MSP/Topham:
11b. Novosti/Science Photo Library: 15tr. Picturepoint/Topham: 17, 19b,
26t, 27c, 28, 29t. Red Blue Green New Media Ltd/Alamy: front cover insert.
Science Photo Library: 25tr. Mitch Wojnarowicz/Image Works/Topham: 14t.

All other photography by Ray Moller.

Published in the United States by Smart Apple Media
2140 Howard Drive West, North Mankato, Minnesota 56003

Library of Congress Cataloging-in-Publication Data

Riley, Peter D.
Materials and matter / by Peter Riley.
p. cm. — (Making sense of science)
Includes index.
ISBN 1-58340-716-2
1. Matter—Juvenile literature. I. Title.

QC173.16.R55 2005
530—dc22   2005043082

2 4 6 8 9 7 5 3 1

CONTENTS

MATERIAL WORLD

Many people think of material as a piece of cloth. It is true that cloth is a material, but wood, metal, pottery, and plastic are materials, too. And the list does not end there. Water, blood, and oil are also materials. The air we breathe, the gas people use for cooking, the scents we smell—all of these are materials. In fact, everything around us is a material of some kind. A material is anything made from what scientists call matter.

The only place where there is no material is in space. Between the stars and the galaxies, there is truly empty space, which contains no matter at all.

Every material on Earth takes one of three forms: solid, liquid, or gas. Solids are objects with definite shapes, such as houses, trees, and books. Liquids, such as water and cooking oil, have no definite shape; they change and flow. Gases are less easy to notice because most of them are invisible. However, we can feel wind, which is the movement of gases in the air, and we can smell the exhaust gases that come from cars. Solid, liquid, and gas are called the three states of matter.

DIFFERENT PROPERTIES

A material's properties make it different from other materials. One property of a solid material is hardness. A rock, for example, is hard, while a sponge is soft. Liquids can differ in viscosity, or how runny they are. Honey and syrup are highly viscous—they flow very slowly—while water, with a low viscosity, flows easily. Most gases, such as oxygen and carbon dioxide, are colorless. However, chlorine, a gas used to make disinfectants, is green.

CHOOSING MATERIALS

For around two million years, people have been taking natural materials and adapting them for their own uses. We use materials with different properties for different purposes. For example, we twist together strands of wool to form yarn, then weave or knit the yarn to make clothes that are comfortable and warm.

Wool would be a very poor material to use for making a coffee mug. But if we moisten clay, mold it, then heat it at high temperatures in a kiln, it makes a hard, waterproof pottery called stoneware—perfect for a coffee mug!

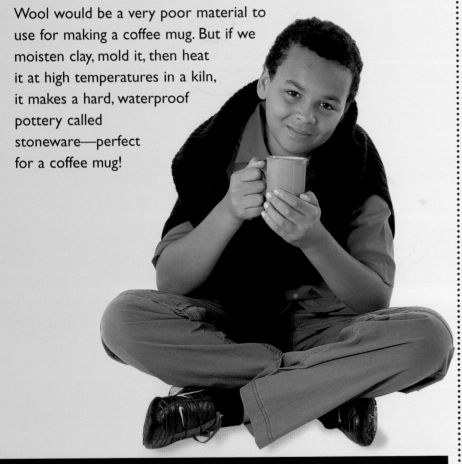

MAKE A BADGE FROM MILK

Alchemists (see the panel below) often warmed and mixed substances to make changes happen. These processes have been a part of chemistry for hundreds of years.

Ask a grown-up to heat about 10 ounces (0.3 l) of milk for you. It must not boil. Add a tablespoon of vinegar and stir. When white lumps appear, separate them from the liquid with a strainer. Squish the lumps together in the strainer to squeeze out more liquid, then form the lump into a disc. Push a safety pin partway into one side of the disc, and leave it to harden. Paint a design on your badge once it has dried.

REAL-LIFE WIZARDS?

One of the first groups of people to extensively study the properties of materials and how they can be changed were alchemists. Alchemy began in ancient Egypt more than 2,000 years ago. Alchemists had two goals: to change ordinary metals into gold and to make a medicine that could give everlasting life. Alchemists accomplished neither of these things, but some of their observations and experiments became part of the science of chemistry, which first developed about 400 years ago.

WHAT IS MATTER?

Tap your head—it is solid matter. Feel your pulse—blood (liquid matter) is being pushed through your body. Breathe in and out—feel the air (gaseous matter) moving in your lungs. We are made of matter, and we live in a material world.

It is difficult to determine what matter really is—there is so much of it! But all matter has two things in common. Matter has mass, and it takes up space.

MASS AND WEIGHT

The mass of an object is the amount of matter it contains. Earth's gravity pulls on this mass with a force called weight. We can feel the weight of solid objects by picking them up (if they are not too heavy), and we can feel the weight of a liquid by comparing a full glass with an empty one. Gases do not seem to have weight, but a simple experiment can show that air has weight and, therefore, also mass.

BALLOON BALANCE

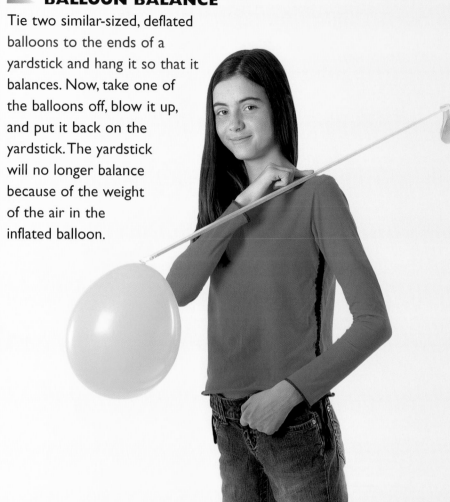

Tie two similar-sized, deflated balloons to the ends of a yardstick and hang it so that it balances. Now, take one of the balloons off, blow it up, and put it back on the yardstick. The yardstick will no longer balance because of the weight of the air in the inflated balloon.

VOLUME

The space taken up by matter is called its volume. You can figure out the volume of a solid, rectangular block of matter by multiplying its length by its width and height. For example, a block of wood one inch (2.5 cm) long, two inches (5 cm) wide, and three inches (7.5 cm) high, has a volume of six cubic inches (94 cu cm). A liquid has no shape, but you can find the volume of a liquid by pouring it into a measuring cup or beaker. To measure the volume of a gas, you can suck it into a syringe.

Using a ruler, a measuring beaker, and a syringe, you can measure the volume of solids, liquids, and gases.

THE VOLUME OF A PEBBLE

You can use a measuring cup to find the volume of an irregular solid object, such as a pebble. Fill a measuring cup half full of water and note the volume. Drop in a pebble, and note the volume again. The pebble's volume is the difference between these two volumes.

DENSITY

The density of a material is a property that combines mass and volume. It is a measure of the mass of a substance in a certain volume. For instance, if a six-cubic-inch (94 cu cm) block of wood has a mass of 10 ounces (300 g), its density is $10 \div 6 = 1.6$ ounce per cubic inch (3.2 g/cu cm).

SEPARATING THE STATES

The properties of volume and density are important in distinguishing between solids, liquids, and gases.
• Solids have a high density, and their volume does not change. They have a definite shape.
• Liquids have a high density, and their volume does not change, but they have no definite shape. Liquids take the shape of whatever container they are in.
• Gases have a low density, and their volume can vary. Gases have no definite shape— they completely fill whatever container they are in.

The volume and density of a solid or a liquid do not change. The volume of a gas can vary and, with it, its density. Air forced into a balloon is more dense than the air around the balloon.

THE **FOUR ELEMENTS**

Thales (642–546 B.C.), a Greek philosopher, believed that all matter was really different forms of a single substance. He called this substance an element. Later, the Greek philosopher Empedocles (c. 490–430 B.C.) stated that matter was made from four elements: air, earth, fire, and water. Different substances were mixtures of different amounts of these four elements. Alchemists used the idea of the four elements in their studies of matter.

PARTICLES OF MATTER

What would you get if you cut a piece of cheese in half, then cut one section in half again, and then took one half of that, and so on? This idea of cutting something up occurred to the ancient Greek philosopher Democritus (470–380 B.C.). He came to the conclusion that, if you continued cutting, you would reach a particle so small that it could not be divided. He called this particle an atom, which means indivisible.

This picture shows the different kinds of atoms and molecules found in air.

= argon   = helium   = oxygen   = carbon dioxide   = nitrogen

Today, we know that matter is made up of tiny particles. The smallest of these are atoms, but there are also other particles, called molecules, made from groups of atoms. All matter is made from atoms or molecules. Some materials are made from just atoms, and some are made from just molecules. Other substances, such as air, are mixtures of different materials and contain both atoms and molecules.

ON THE WAY TO AN ATOM

Tear a piece of paper in half. Take one of the halves and tear it in two. Tear one of the new pieces in half. Continue tearing the paper in this way until the pieces are too small to tear. Atoms are still much smaller than this. There are millions of them in the period at the end of this sentence.

particles in a solid

particles in a liquid

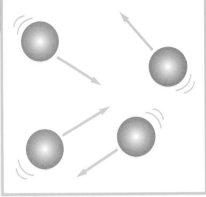
particles in a gas

PARTICLES IN MATTER

The particles in matter help to explain the properties of solids, liquids, and gases.

In solids, the atoms or molecules are tightly packed together. There is very little space between them, so the solid cannot be squished. The particles hold tightly to each other, so the solid keeps its shape. Even though the particles are held in a rigid structure, they vibrate slightly.

The particles in liquids are close together, so, like solids, liquids cannot be compressed. However, the particles are not attached together but can slide over each other. This allows liquid to flow. It also means that liquid does not have a fixed shape. The particles simply flow until they come up against the wall of a container. Then they fill the shape of the container.

The particles in a gas do not hold on to each other in any way. They zoom around in all directions. A gas fills any container it is in. When the container is large, the particles are far apart, but the gas can be squished, like the air in a bicycle tire, so that the particles come closer together.

PEAS AS PARTICLES

Tightly pack some frozen peas into the lid of a coffee jar. The peas are like the particles in a solid. Now, take some peas out and slightly tip the lid so that the peas flow like particles in a liquid. Remove most of the peas and gently shake the lid from side to side. The remaining peas move quickly in all directions like the particles in a gas.

THE PARTICLES THEORY OF MATTER

The idea of matter being made from particles was developed from the study of gases. James Clerk Maxwell (1831–1879) and Ludwig Boltzmann (1844–1906) studied the results of experiments on gases done by other scientists. They found that the behavior of gases could be explained if they were thought of as being made from tiny, fast-moving particles. Since gases can turn into liquids or solids (see pages 10–11), these too must be made of particles.

PHYSICAL CHANGES

Have you ever put a piece of chocolate in your pocket and forgotten about it? In time, the heat from your body changes it from a solid to a sticky liquid. If you put the melted chocolate in a cool place, it turns back to a solid again. These changes show that matter can change its state.

Changes in state are called physical changes. These changes are reversible, as with chocolate.

Material	Melting/freezing point, °F (°C)
water	32 (0)
butter	about 91 (33)
chocolate	about 99 (37)
candle wax	about 140 (60)
nylon	about 482 (250)
lead	620 (327)
gold	1,947 (1,063)
glass	about 2,732 (1,500)
iron	2,800 (1,538)

This table shows the melting or freezing points of some common materials.

PARTICLES IN PHYSICAL CHANGES

The particles in a solid have a little energy, which makes them vibrate. When a solid is heated, it receives more energy, which makes the particles vibrate more. If the particles receive enough energy, they vibrate so much that they break free and slide over each other. This process is called melting. The temperature at which this takes place is the melting point of the solid.

As a liquid cools down, it loses energy. At a certain point, the particles lose so much energy that they can no longer slide over each other; they cling to other particles and vibrate. This is what happens when a liquid freezes. We usually think of freezing as something that happens at low temperatures, as when water freezes. But candle wax, for instance, freezes when it is still warm to the touch. The freezing point of a material is the same as its melting point.

The processes involved when a solid changes to a liquid, then a gas, then back to a solid again.

EVAPORATION

During a rain shower, puddles form, but they do not stay long once the sun comes out. The water disappears by changing from a liquid to a gas in a process called evaporation.

The particles in a liquid slide over each other, but there is still an attraction between the particles that holds them together. However, particles at the surface are held in place only by the liquid particles below them. If the surface particles are moving fast enough, they can break away and form a gas.

HOW FAST DOES WATER EVAPORATE?

Put a saucer of water on a sunny windowsill. Mark the level of the water. After an hour, mark the new water level. Check and record the water level at other times over the next day. Predict when all of it will have evaporated, and see if you are right.

BOILING

When a liquid is heated, many particles evaporate from the surface. Particles within the liquid get enough energy to evaporate as well. These high-energy particles gather to form bubbles of gas, which rise to the surface and pop. When a liquid boils, it is constantly stirred by large gas bubbles forming and popping.

CONDENSATION

Condensation—when a gas cools down and turns into a liquid—is the opposite of evaporation. You can see condensation happening if you breathe on a can of soda from the refrigerator. Droplets of water form on the can as the water vapor in your warm breath condenses on its cold surface.

DRAMATIC SMOKE

If you have been to a rock concert, you may have seen the effect of another physical change. It is called sublimation, and it occurs when a solid turns directly into a gas. Dry ice is solid carbon dioxide. When it is exposed to air, the solid immediately changes to a gas. Energy is used up in this process, and the air becomes colder. Water vapor in the cold air condenses to make clouds that look like smoke.

The "smoke" at this rock concert is actually a cloud of tiny water droplets produced by releasing dry ice.

MIXTURE AND SOLUTIONS

If you get a whiff of perfume or smell newly cut grass, you are smelling something mixed in with the air. Small amounts of perfume or chemicals from the cut grass evaporate and mix with gases in the air. When the scent chemicals reach your nose, you smell them.

Air itself is made up of several different gases (see page 8). When different substances mingle together, they form a mixture. The process of one substance mingling and spreading through another is called diffusion.

WATCHING DIFFUSION

Put a glass dish on top of a piece of graph paper. Fill the dish with cold water, and let it settle. Now, add a drop of food coloring to the water. Time how long it takes for the drop to spread out and cover a particular number of graph squares.

Repeat the experiment with warm water. Does the diffusion happen slower or faster?

OTHER MIXTURES

All kinds of materials form mixtures. Smoke, for instance, is a mixture of hot air (a gas) filled with tiny pieces of soot (a solid). Mist or fog is a mixture of tiny water droplets (a liquid) in air (a gas). Foam is a mixture of a gas in a liquid. The gas is trapped in the liquid and forms bubbles.

Firefighters use foam to put out gas fires. The foam covers the fire like a blanket, while water would make a gas fire spread. For more about burning, see pages 18–19.

These firefighters are using foam to smother the flames of a gas fire.

WHICH LIQUIDS MIX?

Like water, pure alcohol is a colorless liquid. If you mix water and pure alcohol, the result is a colorless mixture. Liquids that mix easily like this are said to be miscible. Some liquids do not mix easily—they are said to be immiscible. Oil and water are immiscible. They do not completely mix together—one liquid forms tiny droplets in the other. This kind of mixture is called an emulsion.

MIXING OIL AND WATER

Stir a tablespoon of cold cooking oil into a beaker of water. Can you make an emulsion?

What happens to the mixture after a few minutes?

SOLUTIONS

A solution is a mixture of a liquid with a solid or a gas, in which the solid or gas completely mixes in and seems to disappear, or dissolve. The liquid part of a solution is called a solvent. Water is the most common solvent.

STIRRING IN SUGAR

Fill two beakers with warm water. Put a teaspoon of sugar in each, but stir only one beaker. Does stirring help the sugar to dissolve? If it does, you will still see sugar crystals in the unstirred liquid, while the sugar in the stirred liquid will have dissolved.

HELPING FISH BREATHE

Gases can form solutions, too. This is very important for fish and other water creatures; it means that oxygen from the air can dissolve in water. This makes it possible for fish to "breathe" underwater.

In aquariums, there is a danger that fish will not get enough oxygen because the tank contains only a small amount of water. To avoid this problem, many aquarium tanks have an air diffuser that pumps air bubbles through the water.

13

SEPARATING MATERIALS

Do your parents like drinking coffee? If they do, they might use a coffeemaker to make it. Hot water and ground coffee beans mix together inside a coffeemaker, but only a clear brown liquid flows into your cup. The coffee solids have been separated from the liquid.

Archaeologists use huge sieves. The soil at a dig is sieved to find small fragments of pottery, small metal objects such as coins, and bones.

SIEVING

A sieve is a fine wire mesh with small holes in it. Large, solid particles can be separated from smaller ones with a sieve. Small particles pass through the sieve, while larger ones are left behind.

A sieve can also be used to separate large solids from a liquid. A cook uses a colander (a kind of sieve) to separate pasta from the water it is cooked in.

FILTERING

Filtering is similar to sieving, but in a filter, the holes are much smaller than in a sieve.

When a mixture is poured into a filter, the liquid passes through the tiny holes, and the solids remain behind. Filters are used in coffeemakers to separate the coffee grounds from the water.

EVAPORATION

Sieving and filtering can separate mixtures, but they cannot separate the parts of a solution. One way to get back a solid dissolved in a liquid is to evaporate the liquid (the solvent). The solvent escapes into the air, and the solid is left behind.

SEPARATING SAND AND SALT

Put some sand and some salt into a beaker of water and stir it. Pour the mixture through a filter to separate out the sand.

Now, put the liquid in a dish on a sunny windowsill, and let the water evaporate. The salt will be left in the bottom of the dish.

You can use a large plastic bottle with the top cut off to hold the filter funnel. Ask a grown-up to cut off the top.

DISTILLATION

When a solution is allowed to evaporate, the solvent is lost into the air. However, sometimes we want to collect the solvent as well as the solid. We can do this by using distillation. In this process, the solution is heated in a flask connected to a tube that is cooled by water. When the solvent evaporates, it rises up into the tube, but because the tube is cooled, the gas condenses and runs into a beaker.

In some coastal places where fresh water is scarce, seawater is distilled to remove the salt and make it fit for drinking.

The pigments (colored chemicals) in several different colored inks have been separated in this paper chromatogram. From left to right, the pigments are black, brown, red, green, blue, and orange.

CHROMATOGRAPHY

Chromatography is a way of separating a mixture of substances in a liquid or a gas. In paper chromatography, a drop of liquid is placed near one end of a piece of filter paper, and the end is dipped in a solvent such as water. The solvent rises through the paper, passes through the spot, and carries the substances upward. The substances travel at different speeds in the solvent and settle in different areas of the paper. If the substances are different colors, like dyes, they can easily be seen.

THE PIGMENTS IN PLANTS

Mikhail Tsvet (1872–1919) was a Russian botanist who wanted to learn more about pigments (colored chemicals) in plants. He developed the earliest kind of chromatography, in which he poured mixtures of plant pigments through a cylinder packed with a special powder.

Different plant pigments traveled different distances down the column and formed bands of colors. Tsvet named the process chromatography after the Greek word for "written in color." It has since been used to help separate and identify many other biologically important materials.

CHEMICAL CHANGES

If you stir sugar into water (see page 13), it disappears, seemingly for good. However, it has only dissolved, and it would be possible to get the sugar back by evaporating the water. But if you put sugar into cookie dough and bake it in the oven, the sugar is changed, and you cannot separate it from the other ingredients. The baking process is a change that cannot be reversed.

All materials are made of tiny particles—atoms or molecules (see page 8). When substances are simply mixed, the different particles mingle but do not change. But in an irreversible change, such as baking, the atoms and molecules in the mixture interact with each other and form new substances. Particles might split apart into smaller particles, or they might join to form bigger particles. These kinds of changes are called chemical reactions.

REACTANTS AND PRODUCTS

The substances that take part in a chemical reaction are called reactants. The new substances produced by the reaction are called products.

One example of a chemical reaction occurs between baking soda and vinegar. This reaction produces bubbles of carbon dioxide gas, and it can be used to make a model of an erupting volcano.

 AN ERUPTING VOLCANO

Put a tablespoon of baking soda in a small plastic bottle. Set the bottle in a tray of sand and build up sand around its sides in the shape of a volcano. Put a drop of red food coloring into half a cup of vinegar, and carefully pour the vinegar into the bottle. Stand back and wait for the eruption.

MAKING CONCRETE

Concrete is a mixture of sand, gravel, cement, and water. When the water mixes with the cement, a chemical reaction takes place. The cement changes from a gray powder into tiny crystals. They bind the sand grains and pieces of gravel to make a strong material used in building.

RUST

The chemical reaction between baking soda and vinegar is fast, but others are much slower. If iron is left in damp surroundings, it gradually begins to rust. Particles of oxygen from the air react with particles of iron and form iron oxide, the red-brown material we call rust.

A piece of rusted iron on a rocky beach. Iron rusts even faster in saltwater than in freshwater.

HOW LONG DOES RUST TAKE?

Wrap some iron nails in a wet paper towel and put them in a plastic bag. Seal the bag, but check the nails every day for signs of rust. Repeat the experiment with two bags of damp nails. Put one in a cold place, such as the refrigerator, and one in a warm place, such as a cupboard. Predict which will rust first, then test your prediction.

FROM GASES TO FERTILIZER

Chemical reactions do not take place only between solids and liquids—they can take place between gases, too. In 1908, Fritz Haber (1868–1934), a German chemist, built an apparatus for creating ammonia by mixing hydrogen and nitrogen gases. In 1913, German scientist Carl Bosch (1874–1940) built a chemical plant, or factory, for making ammonia in large quantities. Ammonia is still made in chemical plants today. Nitrogen and hydrogen gases are heated and compacted until the reaction that produces ammonia takes place. Ammonia has many uses, including making fertilizer. Part of your lunch may have been grown with the help of fertilizer made in an ammonia plant.

17

Burning is a spectacular chemical reaction, but it can be dangerous. Large amounts of heat are given off, which can cause other materials to catch fire. When certain materials burn, they produce poisonous fumes. Burning is a reaction that must be treated with great care.

Materials that burn are called fuels. A fuel usually has to be heated before it will burn, but once it starts burning, it gives off more heat.

A BURNING CANDLE

The fuel in a candle is wax, which is made from hydrogen and carbon. When a candle burns, the wax takes part in a reaction with oxygen that produces carbon dioxide and water vapor. Both products are gases and mix with the air.

A CAMPFIRE

Many people enjoy a campfire. Wood is made from carbon and hydrogen, but there are other substances present, too. When wood burns, the carbon and hydrogen react with oxygen to form carbon dioxide and water vapor, just as in a candle. But some of the other materials do not burn; they are left behind and form ash. Ash is rich in simple chemicals called minerals. Plants need minerals to help them grow, so if the ash is added to soil, it will help new plants to grow.

A fire that is out of control can cause great damage and injury.

THE TRIANGLE OF FIRE

A fire needs three things to burn: oxygen, fuel, and heat. This is known as the triangle of fire. If any one of these is removed, the fire will go out.

The triangle of fire is useful when fighting fires. Foresters leave wide gaps between stands of trees to stop fires from spreading. Trees are the fuel in a forest fire, so if a gap is left, there is no fuel for the fire, and it will go out. Fire engines pump water onto a fire to cool it and put it out. Some fire extinguishers produce a foam (see page 13), which smothers fires and prevents oxygen from getting to them.

MAKE A FIRE EXTINGUISHER

Set a candle in a tray of sand. Ask a grown-up to light it. Pour half a cup of vinegar into a jug, add a teaspoon of baking soda, and let the mixture fizz. Carbon dioxide, which is heavier than air, will collect in the jug. Carefully tip the jug so the carbon dioxide spreads over the candle, but no liquid spills out. The carbon dioxide keeps oxygen from reaching the flame, so the candle should go out.

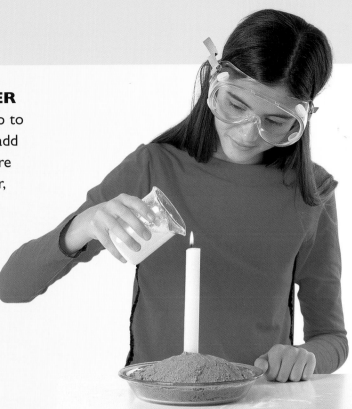

EXTINGUISHING A THEORY

When wood burns, it leaves only a small amount of ash. For many years, scientists wondered what happened to the rest of the wood, which seemed to disappear. Georg Stahl (1660–1734), a German doctor, believed that when something burned, a substance that he called phlogiston escaped into the air. Scientists accepted the phlogiston theory for more than 100 years.

According to the phlogiston theory, all substances heated in air lose weight. However, experiments showed that some substances actually gain weight when they burn. Antoine Lavoisier (1743–1794), a French scientist, studied these burning experiments and repeated them. His work led to the discovery that when something burns, oxygen combines with the fuel to form an oxide.

When wood burns, the oxide (carbon dioxide) is a gas and mixes with the air. But other fuels burn to form solid oxides, and the oxygen added to the fuel increases its weight after burning.

Antoine Lavoisier.

Imagine that you are an alchemist living nearly 400 years ago. You are looking for a substance called the philosopher's stone, which you believe can give eternal life and change ordinary metals into gold. You have heated many things but have not found anything new. In desperation, you decide to heat urine. When the smelly fumes clear away, you are left with a white, waxy substance. When you place it in the dark, you are amazed to see that it glows.

This story actually happened; the alchemist was a German named Hennig Brand. He did not find the philosopher's stone, but he was the first person to discover a new element. Brand called the substance phosphorus, which means "light bearer."

WHAT IS AN ELEMENT?

There are millions of different materials—too many to count—but there are only slightly more than 100 elements. Elements are materials made from just one kind of atom.

Elements are the building blocks for other materials. They combine in a huge variety of ways to form all of the other substances that exist. (See page 23 for more information on some of the compounds made from elements.)

	1	2	3	4	5	6	7	8	9
1	1 H Hydrogen								
2	3 Li Lithium	4 Be Beryllium							
3	11 Na Sodium	12 Mg Magnesium							
4	19 K Potassium	20 Ca Calcium	21 Sc Scandium	22 Ti Titanium	23 V Vanadium	24 Cr Chromium	25 Mn Manganese	26 Fe Iron	27 Co Cobalt
5	37 Rb Rubidium	38 Sr Strontium	39 Y Yttrium	40 Zr Zirconium	41 Nb Niobium	42 Mo Molybdenum	43 Tc Technetium	44 Ru Ruthenium	45 Rh Rhodium
6	55 Cs Caesium	56 Ba Barium		72 Hf Hafnium	73 Ta Tantalum	74 W Tungsten	75 Re Rhenium	76 Os Osmium	77 Ir Iridium
7	87 Fr Francium	88 Ra Radium		104 Rf Rutherfordium	105 Db Dubnium	106 Sg Seaborgium	107 Bh Bohrium	108 Hs Hassium	109 Mt Meitnerium
				57 La Lanthanum	58 Ce Cerium	59 Pr Praseodymium	60 Nd Neodymium	61 Pm Promethium	62 Sm Samarium
				89 Ac Actinium	90 Th Thorium	91 Pa Protactinium	92 U Uranium	93 Np Neptunium	94 Pu Plutonium

John Dalton (1766–1844), an English chemist, studied how elements joined together to make compounds by weighing the elements and the compounds they formed. He found that each element had a particular atomic weight, and he made a list of the elements in order of their atomic weights.

Dmitri Mendeleev (1834–1907), a Russian chemist, noticed that when the elements were arranged in order of atomic weight, elements with similar properties occurred at regular intervals down the list. He arranged the elements into a table called the periodic table, which grouped elements with similar properties in the same column. Scientists still use a version of the periodic table today.

THE PERIODIC TABLE

Through the studies by Dmitri Mendeleev and others (see panel), scientists realized that elements could be arranged into groups. They were organized into a table called the periodic table, in which elements in the same group, or column, have similar properties. Each element has a one- or two-letter symbol as well as a name. (Find out more about these symbols on page 23.)

Elements in the same group in the periodic table have similar properties. For example, all of the gases in the same column as helium do not react chemically with other elements.

							2 He Helium
			5 B Boron	6 C Carbon	7 N Nitrogen	8 O Oxygen	9 F Fluorine	10 Ne Neon
			13 Al Aluminium	14 Si Silicon	15 P Phosphorous	16 S Sulphur	17 Cl Chlorine	18 Ar Argon
28 Ni Nickel	29 Cu Copper	30 Zn Zinc	31 Ga Gallium	32 Ge Germanium	33 As Arsenic	34 Se Selenium	35 Br Bromine	36 Kr Krypton
46 Pd Palladium	47 Ag Silver	48 Cd Cadmium	49 In Indium	50 Sn Tin	51 Sb Antimony	52 Te Tellurium	53 I Iodine	54 Xe Xenon
78 Pt Platinum	79 Au Gold	80 Hg Mercury	81 Tl Thallium	82 Pb Lead	83 Bi Bismuth	84 Po Polonium	85 At Astatine	86 Rn Radon
110 Uun Ununnilium	111 Uuu Unununnium	112 Uub Ununbium						

63 Eu Europium	64 Gd Gadolinium	65 Tb Terbium	66 Dy Dysprosium	67 Ho Holmium	68 Er Erbium	69 Tm Thulium	70 Yb Ytterbium	71 Lu Lutetium
95 Am Americium	96 Cm Curium	97 Bk Berkelium	98 Cf Californium	99 Es Einsteinium	100 Fm Fermium	101 Md Mendelevium	102 No Nobelium	103 Lr Lawrencium
10	11	12	13	14	15	16	17	18

ATOMS AND COMPOUNDS

Look at a ruler and find the millimeter marks. The ruler cannot measure atoms, but it can give an idea of how small they are. About 10 million atoms would fit in 1 millimeter on a ruler.

Scientists used to think of atoms as tiny, hard spheres. They thought atoms could not be divided into anything smaller. However, today we know that atoms are made up of smaller particles called subatomic particles.

INSIDE AN ATOM

An atom has two main parts. In the center is a small nucleus made of particles called protons and neutrons. Moving around the nucleus at high speeds are much tinier particles called electrons.

Electrons have a negative electrical charge, and protons have a positive electrical charge. The electrical charges balance because the number of electrons is the same as the number of protons. Neutrons do not have an electrical charge.

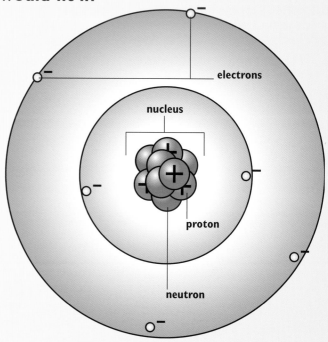

Different elements have different numbers of protons in their nucleus. Hydrogen has one proton, helium has two, and so on. This coincides with their number on the periodic table (see page 20).

MAKE A SIMPLE ATOM

Ask a grown-up to cut a large orange in half. Remove the flesh of the orange, leaving two hollow skins. Attach a ball of clay to a fine strand of thread. Using a needle, pull the thread through the top of one of the skins. Let the thread hang down so the end is in the center of the hollow. Secure the thread to the top of the skin with tape.

The clay represents the nucleus, the hollow is the space inside the atom, and the skin represents the outer limit of the atom, where some electrons zoom around. Join the two halves of the skin to make the "atom" complete.

This model of the atom is not to scale. If the nucleus really was this size, the atom would be as wide as four school buses!

COMPOUNDS

Atoms of different elements join together through chemical reactions to make compounds.

Each element has its own properties. When elements join to make a compound, the compound has different properties than those of the two elements. For example, carbon is a black solid. There is carbon in fuels such as coal and charcoal. Oxygen is a gas that causes things to burn. When coal is burned, carbon and oxygen atoms join to make the compound carbon dioxide. This is a colorless gas that does not allow things to burn in it.

sodium   chlorine

These salt crystals have square shapes because sodium and chlorine atoms join together in regular cubes (see inset diagram).

TYPES OF COMPOUNDS

When some atoms form compounds, they stack together in a regular way to make a structure called a lattice. Common salt is one such compound. It is made from the elements sodium and chlorine.

Atoms can also join by sharing their electrons. When they do this, they form molecules. Water is made from two atoms of hydrogen and one atom of oxygen.

When chemists want to record a chemical reaction, they do not draw pictures or write words—they use the symbols on the periodic table (page 20). They use numbers to show how many atoms of each element are in a compound. For instance, carbon dioxide, which has one carbon atom and two oxygen atoms is written CO_2.

The description of a chemical reaction using symbols is called an equation. The substances on the left of the equation are called reactants, and the substances on the right are called products.

This is the equation for carbon and oxygen forming carbon dioxide: $C + O_2 \rightarrow CO_2$.

oxygen

hydrogen   hydrogen

The structure of a water molecule. It is written H_2O.

23

ACIDS AND ALKALIS

What do you think of when you think of an acid? Chances are, you will think of a dangerous liquid that fumes and can burn your skin. Some acids are indeed like this. Others, such as citric acid, are present in foods such as oranges and grapes.

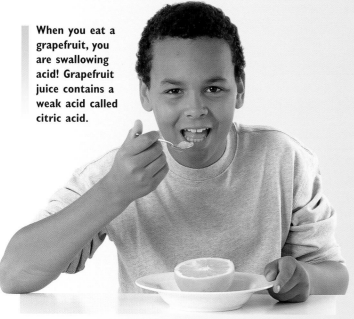

When you eat a grapefruit, you are swallowing acid! Grapefruit juice contains a weak acid called citric acid.

Alkali is a word you may not have used before. In one way, an alkali is the opposite of an acid. Like acids, there are some alkalis that are safe enough to eat—the baking soda that people use to make cakes rise is an alkali. But alkalis can be just as dangerous as acids. Some alkalis can turn the fat layer of your skin into soap!

HELPFUL ALKALIS

Alkalis are used in the chemical industry to make many useful products. One powerful alkali, sodium hydroxide, is mixed with fats and oils from animals and plants to make soap. Sodium hydroxide is also used in making paper, rubber dyes, and bleach. Another alkali, sodium carbonate, is used in making bath crystals and detergents.

ACIDS AND ALCHEMY

Jabir ibn-Hayyan was also known as Abu Musa. His name appears on more than 2,000 books, but scholars do not think that he wrote all of them.

Jabir ibn-Hayyan (about 760–815), an Arabian alchemist, used the process of distillation (see page 15) to make a strong acid from vinegar. He also made nitric acid, which is used today to make fertilizer, medicines, and fibers for cloth.

Hard soaps are made using sodium hydroxide and vegetable oils. But if you used potassium hydroxide instead, you would get liquid soap.

INDICATORS

Acids and alkalis are often colorless liquids, like water. However, we can tell them apart using substances called indicators. An indicator changes color when an acid or an alkali is present. The best-known indicator is called litmus paper. There are two kinds. Blue litmus paper is used to test for acids—it turns red when it is dipped in an acid. Red litmus paper tests for alkalis, and turns blue when dipped in an alkali.

A more useful indicator is called universal indicator paper. It shows a range of colors depending on the strength of the acid or alkali. Strong acids turn it red, weaker acids turn it pink, orange, or yellow. Strong alkalis turn universal indicator paper purple, while weaker alkalis turn it lilac or blue.

A liquid that is neither acid nor alkali is said to be neutral. Pure water is neutral and turns universal indicator paper green.

TESTING FOR ACIDS AND ALKALIS

We can use an indicator to test if household materials are acids or alkalis. Wear rubber gloves and safety glasses for this experiment, as some cleaning materials can hurt your skin and eyes.

Put small amounts of lemon juice, vinegar, baking soda dissolved in water, liquid hand soap, salt dissolved in water, and plain water in separate plastic cups. Test each liquid with universal indicator paper. Which is the most acidic? Which is the most alkaline? Are any of the liquids neutral?

NEUTRALIZATION

When an acid and an alkali are mixed in equal amounts, a chemical reaction called neutralization takes place. The acidity of the acid and the alkalinity of the alkali cancel each other out. The result is a neutral compound called a salt. The salt we put in food (sodium chloride) is only one of many different salts.

The reaction between baking soda and vinegar (see page 16) is a neutralization reaction. Baking soda is an alkali (sodium carbonate), and vinegar contains ethanoic acid. When they react together, they form the salt sodium ethanoate, plus carbon dioxide and water.

USING MATERIALS

Imagine you are a castaway on a desert island. How would you make your home? You might use driftwood from the beach to make the framework of a hut, then cover the framework with huge palm leaves. You could use "string" made from the long stems of plants to hold the palm leaves in place.

In time, you would probably learn to use other materials, such as rocks to make tools, and shells for cups. You would be using materials to survive, as people have done for two million years.

NATURAL OR MANUFACTURED

We can divide materials into two groups according to where they come from. If they come from the world around us, such as wood, stone, or wool, they are natural materials. If they come from a factory, such as pottery, they are manufactured materials. When a natural material is used to make a manufactured material, it is called a raw material. For example, clay is a raw material used to make pottery.

Pottery is one of the oldest manufactured materials. This small vase was made in Greece nearly 2,000 years ago.

METALS

Only a few metals (gold, silver, and copper) are found naturally as pure metal. Other metals are found in rocks, combined with other substances. Metal-rich rocks of this kind are called ores. In iron ore, for example, iron is combined with oxygen as iron oxide.

Ores are often heated to separate the metal from the rock. Iron can be separated from oxygen by heating it in a blast furnace. Crushed iron ore is put into the blast furnace along with coke and limestone. Jets of very hot air heat everything up. As the coke burns, carbon atoms combine with oxygen from the air to make carbon monoxide. This gas takes part in a chemical reaction with the iron oxide to make carbon dioxide, leaving behind iron.

A cutaway picture of a blast furnace.

iron ore, coke, and limestone

930 °F (500 °C)

1,560 °F (850 °C)

1,830 °F (1000 °C)

2,370 °F (1300 °C)

3,450 °F (1,900 °C)

waste gases

very hot air

slag (waste)

molten iron

26

Iron from a blast furnace is not pure: it contains large amounts of carbon. A more useful material can be made by removing most of the carbon. To do this, oxygen is blasted through the hot metal. The oxygen combines with the carbon to make carbon dioxide and carbon monoxide. The metal that is produced is steel. Steel has a wide variety of uses, from car bodies to paper clips.

An oil refinery. Many of the tall structures are distillation towers where the different chemicals in oil, called hydrocarbons, are separated.

PLASTICS

Plastics are among today's most useful manufactured materials. They are usually made from oil, which is a mixture of hydrocarbons. A hydrocarbon is a chain of carbon atoms with hydrogen atoms attached.

The different hydrocarbons in oil are separated by a special kind of distillation at an oil refinery. To make plastics, small hydrocarbon molecules are joined together into long chains. Sometimes other elements are added as well; for instance, PVC (polyvinyl chloride) contains the element chlorine.

PAPER-MAKING

Paper was invented in China slightly over 2,000 years ago. It was originally made from hemp plants, which were mashed in water, then laid on mats to dry. Later, the bark of the mulberry tree was used. Today, we use the fibers from wood to make paper. We also recycle paper by mashing it and using it again.

MAKE RECYCLED PAPER

Cut some paper into short, narrow strips. Mash the strips in water to make a pulp. Spread a thin layer of pulp on a piece of fine wire netting or a metal grid with small spaces (for example, a cooling tray for baking). Use a rolling pin to squeeze out some of the water, then leave the pulp to dry. How does it compare with manufactured paper?

CHEMICALS IN THE ENVIRONMENT

If you look around, you will find chemicals everywhere. You see everything around you through a gaseous mixture of chemicals—the air. Your chair may be made of metal and plastic or wood and fabric. If you are outside, you may be sitting on grass or stone. All of these are made of chemicals.

Not only nonliving things are made of chemicals. Plants, animals, and humans are like living chemistry sets. Almost everything around us is taking part in chemical reactions.

BODY CHEMISTRY

Your body is made from a great many compounds and elements that keep you alive. Your bones are made from calcium compounds, and your muscles are made from protein. Your stomach produces a strong acid that kills germs and helps to break down food. And a slimy chemical, called mucin, stops the acid from burning the walls of your stomach.

Chemicals produce the energy you need to do things, and they are used up as the body grows and repairs itself. To replace the chemicals that are used up, we eat food. If you eat a balanced diet, you supply your body with all the chemicals it needs to stay healthy.

The chemical reactions that keep you alive produce wastes that you must get rid of. For example, carbon dioxide is a waste that is released when you breathe out.

Calcium is an important chemical for the body. If there is too little calcium in your diet, your body takes some from your bones, which may become weak and brittle. This X ray shows the bones in a hand, one of which has been damaged by disease.

HOW WET ARE YOU?

A human body is about 65 percent water. To find out how heavy the water in your body is, weigh yourself, divide the answer by 100, then multiply by 65.

ENVIRONMENTAL DAMAGE

We use materials from the environment to make useful objects such as chairs and computers. We also use fuels such as coal, oil, and gas to heat our homes or to generate electricity at a power station. Collecting these natural materials can cause environmental damage. For example, we cut down forests for wood to make paper or to build houses, and we dig huge holes in the ground to mine metals and coal.

We also damage the environment when we burn fuels or turn raw materials into manufactured materials. For example, chemicals such as soot and sulphur dioxide may be released into the air when fuel is burned in a power station. The sulphur dioxide can then dissolve in falling rain and make the rain more acidic. Acid rain and soot can damage living things and destroy habitats.

The older, larger trees in this forest have been badly damaged by acid rain. Slowly, new trees are growing beneath them, and the forest is regenerating.

TESTING THE RAIN

Paint a piece of wood white, and let the paint dry. Next time it rains, put the wood outside for half an hour, then examine it for soot particles with a magnifying glass. Is there soot in the rain? Collect some rainwater in a bowl, and use universal indicator paper to test its acidity. Rain is usually a very weak acid, but pollution can make it dangerously acidic.

Many areas of rain forest have been cut down for wood or to make space for farming. In some areas, workers are trying to restore the forest.

ARE MATERIALS RUNNING OUT?

Some materials, such as wool and wood, are renewable. When you shear a sheep, it grows more wool, and when you chop down trees, you can plant seeds that will grow into new trees.

Materials such as metals and oil are nonrenewable. There are certain amounts of these materials on Earth, and, in time, they will run out. To prevent this from happening, materials such as paper, metals, and glass are being recycled so that fewer supplies have to be taken from Earth.

Recycling can save materials for the future and reduce environmental damage. But we still need to do more to prevent raw materials from eventually running out.

29

TIMELINE

2 million–5500 years ago, the Stone Age. People did not know about metals at this time. Axes, knives, and other tools and weapons were made from stone.

3500–2500 B.C., the Bronze Age. Bronze (a metal made from tin and copper) was discovered, and many tools and weapons were made from it.

2500 B.C.–A.D. 500, the Iron Age. Iron, which is much stronger than bronze, was used for making tools and weapons.

Note: The time of the Stone, Bronze, and Iron Ages varies from place to place. In the 20th century, some rain forest communities still followed a Stone Age way of life.

c. 2000 B.C., alchemy began in Egypt.

Thales (642–546 B.C.), a Greek philosopher, thought that all matter was made from one element.

Empedocles (c. 490–430 B.C.), a Greek philosopher, believed that matter consisted of air, earth, fire, and water.

Democritus (470–380 B.C.), a Greek philosopher, thought that matter was made up of tiny particles called atoms.

Jabir ibn-Hayyan (c. A.D. 760–815), an Arabian alchemist, made nitric acid.

Robert Boyle (1627–1691), a British scientist, believed that an element was something that could not be broken down into simpler substances.

Georg Stahl (1660–1734), a German doctor, presented the phlogiston theory, which said that burning materials gave out phlogiston into the air.

Antoine Lavoisier (1743–1794), a French scientist, proved the phlogiston theory wrong and showed that when materials burned, they combined with oxygen from the air.

John Dalton (1766–1844), an English chemist, discovered that each element had an atomic weight.

James Clerk Maxwell (1831–1879), a Scottish scientist, developed the idea of matter being made from particles. With Ludwig Bolzmann (see below), he used this idea to explain the behavior of gases.

Dmitri Mendeleev (1834–1907), a Russian chemist, devised the periodic table of elements.

Ludwig Boltzmann (1844–1906), an Austrian scientist, further developed the idea of matter being made from particles. With James Clerk Maxwell (see above), he used this idea to explain the behavior of gases.

Fritz Haber (1868–1934), a German chemist, made an apparatus in which hydrogen and nitrogen gases formed ammonia gas.

Michael Tsvet (1872–1919), a Russian botanist, invented chromatography.

Carl Bosch (1874–1940), a German scientist, built a factory in which ammonia could be made from hydrogen and nitrogen.

GLOSSARY

acid – a liquid that turns blue litmus paper red. Lemon juice and vinegar are weak acids. Some acids are dangerous and can burn the skin.

adapting – changing something so that it can perform a useful purpose.

alkali – a liquid that turns red litmus paper blue. Baking soda is an alkali, but some alkalis are dangerous.

atoms – very tiny particles that make up all materials.

condensation – a process during which a gas cools so much that it turns into a liquid.

diffusion – a process in which the particles of two gases or two liquids mix together without being stirred.

distillation – a process in which a solution is separated, and the liquid or liquids that make up the solution are collected.

electron – A tiny particle in an atom that has a negative electrical charge.

element – a substance formed from one type of atom. Chemical reactions cannot break down an element into a simpler substance.

emulsion – a mixture of two liquids, one of which forms tiny droplets in the other.

evaporation – a process in which a liquid changes into a gas.

habitat – the place where a plant or an animal lives.

hydrocarbon – a molecule made from hydrogen and carbon atoms.

immiscible – a property of a liquid that prevents it from mixing with another liquid.

matter – the "stuff" that everything is made of; anything that has mass.

miscible – a property of a liquid that allows it to mix with another liquid.

molecule – a group of atoms joined together.

neutron – a particle in the nucleus of an atom that does not have an electrical charge.

periodic table – a table in which the chemical elements are arranged in order of increasing atomic number (the number of protons in the nucleus). All of the elements in the same group, or column, in the periodic table have similar properties.

philosopher – a person who thinks about things and who uses reason and argument to explain his or her surroundings.

proton – a particle in the nucleus of an atom that has a positive electrical charge.

solution – a liquid in which other substances are dissolved.

solvent – a liquid capable of dissolving a substance.

state – a condition in which matter exists (solid, liquid, or gas).

vibrate – to move rapidly from side to side or up and down.

water vapor – water in the form of a gas in the air.

INDEX